T0022921

ASTROLOGY
SELF-CARE

# Taurus

# ASTROLOGY
# SELF-CARE

# Taurus

## Live your best life
## by the stars

*Sarah Bartlett*

First published in Great Britain in 2022 by Yellow Kite
An imprint of Hodder & Stoughton
An Hachette UK company

1

Copyright © Sarah Bartlett 2022

The right of Sarah Bartlett to be identified as the Author
of the Work has been asserted by her in accordance
with the Copyright, Designs and Patents Act 1988.

All rights reserved. No part of this publication may be reproduced,
stored in a retrieval system, or transmitted, in any form or by any
means without the prior written permission of the publisher,
nor be otherwise circulated in any form of binding or cover
other than that in which it is published and without a similar
condition being imposed on the subsequent purchaser.

Illustrations © shutterstock.com

A CIP catalogue record for this title is
available from the British Library

Hardback ISBN 978 1 399 70461 8
eBook ISBN 978 1 399 70462 5
Audiobook ISBN 978 1 399 70463 2

Designed by Goldust Design

Typeset in Nocturne Serif by Hewer Text UK Ltd, Edinburgh
Printed and bound in Great Britain by Clays Ltd, Elcograf S.p.A.

Hodder & Stoughton policy is to use papers that are
natural, renewable and recyclable products and made
from wood grown in sustainable forests. The logging and
manufacturing processes are expected to conform to the
environmental regulations of the country of origin.

Yellow Kite
Hodder & Stoughton Ltd
Carmelite House
50 Victoria Embankment
London EC4Y 0DZ

www.yellowkitebooks.co.uk

*And the day came when the risk to remain tight in a bud was more painful than the risk it took to blossom.*

Anaïs Nin, diarist and writer

*There is a path, hidden between the road of reason and the hedgerow of dreams, which leads to the secret garden of self-knowledge. This book will show you the way.*

# Contents

Introduction                              11

The Taurus Personality                    29

Caring For Your Mind And Feelings         37

Caring For Your Body                      69

Caring For Your Soul                      97

Last Words                               107

Resources                                109

Glossary                                 111

# Introduction

The ancient Greek goddess Gaia arose from Chaos and was the personification of the Earth and all of Nature. One of the first primordial beings, along with Tartarus (the Underworld), Eros (love) and Nyx (night), as mother of all life, she is both the embodiment of all that this planet is and its spiritual caretaker.

It's hardly likely you will want to become a full-time Mother Earth, but many of us right now are caring more about our beautiful planet and all that lives upon it. To nurture and respect this amazing place we call home, and to preserve this tiny dot in the Universe, the best place to start is, well, with you.

Self-care is about respecting and honouring who you are as an individual. It's about realising that nurturing yourself is neither vanity nor a conceit, but a creative act that brings an awesome sense of awareness and a deeper connection to the Universe and all that's in it. Caring about yourself means you care about everything in the cosmos – because you are part of it.

But self-care isn't just about trekking to the gym, jogging around the park or eating the right foods. It's also about discovering who you are becoming as an individual and caring for that authenticity (and loving and caring about who we are becoming means others can love and care about us, too). This is where the art of sun-sign astrology comes in.

# Astrology and Self-Care

So what is astrology? And how can it direct each of us to the right self-care pathway? Put simply, astrology is the study of the planets, sun and moon and their influence on events and people here on Earth. It is an art that has been used for thousands of years to forecast world events, military and political outcomes and, more recently, financial market trends. As such, it is an invaluable tool for understanding our own individuality and how to be true to ourselves. Although there is still dispute within astrological circles as to whether the planets actually physically affect us, there is strong evidence to show that the cycles and patterns they create in the sky have a direct mirroring effect on what happens down here on Earth and, more importantly, on each individual's personality.

Your horoscope or birth-chart is a snapshot of the planets, sun and moon in the sky at the moment you were born. This amazing picture reveals all your innate potential, characteristics and qualities. In fact, it is probably the best 'selfie' you could ever have! Astrology can not only tell you who you are, but also how best to care for that self and your own specific needs and desires as revealed by your birth-chart.

Self-care is simply time to look after yourself – to restore, inspirit and refresh and love your unique self. But it's also about understanding, accepting and

13

being aware of your own traits – both the good and not so good – so that you can then say, 'It's ok to be me, and my intention is to become the best of myself'. In fact, by looking up to the stars and seeing how they reflect us down here on Earth, we can deepen our connection to the Universe for the good of all, too. Understanding that caring about ourselves is not selfish creates an awesome sense of self-acceptance and awareness.

So how does each of us honour the individual 'me' and find the right kind of rituals and practices to suit our personalities? Astrology sorts us out into the zodiac – an imaginary belt encircling the Earth divided into twelve sun signs; so, for example, what one sign finds relaxing, another may find a hassle or stressful. When it comes to physical fitness, adventurous Arians thrive on aerobic work, while soulful Pisceans feel nurtured by yoga. Financial reward or status would inspire the ambitious Capricorn mind, while theatrical Leos need to indulge their joy of being centre stage.

By knowing which sun sign you are and its associated characteristics, you will discover the right self-care routines and practices to suit you. And this unique and empowering book is here to help – with all the rituals and practices in these pages specifically suited to your sun-sign personality for nurturing and vitalising your mind, body and spirit.

However, self-care is not an excuse to be lazy and avoid the goings on in the rest of the world. Self-care is about taking responsibility for our choices and understanding our unique essence, so that we can engage with all aspects of ourselves and the way we interact with the world.

## IN A NUTSHELL

The Bull is a creature of habit, so any physical indulgence in looking after the self is a delight for this most earthy and sensual sign of the zodiac. This book will not only bring you new ideas to enjoy, but also boost your self-awareness and understanding of who you truly are. Your potential for managing and shaping your creativity into something tangible is going to be the most important aspect of Taurus self-care, so that you can begin to appreciate and nurture your own talents. So love your creativity, show it off to the world and the world will love you in return.

# Sun-Sign Astrology

Also known as your star sign or zodiac sign, your sun sign encompasses the following:

* Your solar identity, or sense of self
* What really matters to you
* Your future intentions
* Your sense of purpose
* Various qualities that manifest through your actions, goals, desires and the personal sense of being 'you'
* Your sense of being 'centred' – whether 'self-centred' (too much ego) or 'self-conscious' (too little ego); in other words, how you perceive who you are as an individual

In fact, the sun tells you how you can 'shine' best to become who you really are.

# ASTROLOGY FACTS

The zodiac or sun signs are twelve 30-degree segments that create an imaginary belt around the Earth. The zodiac belt is also known as the ecliptic, which is the apparent path of the sun as it travels round the Earth during the year.

The sun or zodiac signs are further divided into four elements (Fire, Earth, Air and Water, denoting a certain energy ruling each sign), plus three modalities (qualities associated with how we interact with the world; these are known as Cardinal, Fixed and Mutable). So as a Taurean, for example, you are a 'Fixed Earth' sign.

* Fire signs: Aries, Leo, Sagittarius
  They are: extrovert, passionate, assertive

* Earth signs: Taurus, Virgo, Capricorn
  They are: practical, materialistic, sensual

* Air signs: Gemini, Libra, Aquarius
  They are: communicative, innovative, inquisitive

* Water signs: Cancer, Scorpio, Pisces
  They are: emotional, intuitive, understanding

The modalities are based on their seasonal resonance according to the northern hemisphere.

Cardinal signs instigate and initiate ideas and projects.
They are: Aries, Cancer, Libra and Capricorn

Fixed signs resolutely build and shape ideas.
They are: Taurus, Leo, Scorpio and Aquarius

Mutable signs generate creative change and adapt
ideas to reach a conclusion.
They are: Gemini, Virgo, Sagittarius and Pisces

## Planetary rulers

Each zodiac sign is assigned a planet, which
highlights the qualities of that sign:

Aries is ruled by Mars (fearless)
Taurus is ruled by Venus (indulgent)
Gemini is ruled by Mercury (magical)
Cancer is ruled by the moon (instinctive)
Leo is ruled by the sun (empowering)
Virgo is ruled by Mercury (informative)
Libra is ruled by Venus (compassionate)
Scorpio is ruled by Pluto (passionate)
Sagittarius is ruled by Jupiter (adventurous)
Capricorn is ruled by Saturn (disciplined)
Aquarius is ruled by Uranus (innovative)
Pisces is ruled by Neptune (imaginative)

# Opposite Signs

Signs oppose one another across the zodiac (i.e. those that are 180 degrees away from each other) – for example, Taurus opposes Scorpio and Aries opposes Libra. We often find ourselves mysteriously attracted to our opposite signs in romantic relationships, and while the signs' traits appear to clash in this 'polarity', the essence of each is contained in the other (note, they have the same modality). Gaining insight into the characteristics of your opposite sign (which are, essentially, inherent in you) can deepen your understanding of the energetic interplay of the horoscope.

# On The Cusp

Some of us are born 'on the cusp' of two signs – in other words, the day or time when the sun moved from one zodiac sign to another. If you were born at the end or beginning of the dates usually given in horoscope pages (the sun's move through one sign usually lasts approximately four weeks), you can check which sign you are by contacting a reputable astrologer (or astrology site) (see Resources, p. 109) who will calculate it exactly for you. For example, 23 August is the standardised changeover day for the sun to move into Virgo and out of Leo. But every year, the time and even sometimes the day the sun changes sign can differ. So, say you were born on 23 August at five in the morning and the sun didn't move into Virgo until five in the afternoon on that day, you would be a Leo, not a Virgo.

# How To Use This Book

The book is divided into three parts, each guiding you in applying self-care to different areas of your life:

* Part One: your mind and feelings
* Part Two: your body
* Part Three: your soul

Caring about the mind using rituals or ideas tailored to your sign shows you ways to unlock stress, restore focus or widen your perception. Applying the practices in Part One will connect you to your feelings and help you to acknowledge and become aware of why your emotions are as they are and how to deal with them. This sort of emotional self-care will set you up to deal with your relationships better, enhance all forms of communication and ensure you know exactly how to ask for what you want or need, and be true to your deepest desires.

21

# A WORD ON CHAKRAS

Eastern spiritual traditions maintain that universal energy, known as 'prana' in India and 'chi' in Chinese philosophy, flows through the body, linked by seven subtle energy centres known as chakras (Sanskrit for 'wheel'). These energies are believed to revolve or spiral around and through our bodies, vibrating at different frequencies (corresponding to seven colours of the light spectrum) in an upward, vertical direction. Specific crystals are placed on the chakras to heal, harmonise, stimulate or subdue the chakras if imbalance is found.

The seven chakras are:
* The base or root (found at the base of the spine)
* The sacral (mid-belly)
* The solar plexus (between belly and chest)
* The heart (centre of chest)
* The throat (throat)
* The third eye (between the eyebrows)
* The crown (top of the head)

On p. 91 we will look in more detail at how Taureans can work with chakras for self-care.

Fitness and caring for the body are different for all of us, too. While Taurus benefits from aromatherapy, for example, Sagittarius prefers to go for a run, and Gemini a daily quick stretch or yoga. Delve into Part Two whenever you're in need of physical restoration or a sensual makeover tailored to your sign.

Spiritual self-care opens you to your sacred self or soul. Which is why Part Three looks at how you can nurture your soul according to your astrological sun sign. It shows you how to connect to and care for your spirituality in simple ways, such as being at one with Nature or just enjoying the world around you. It will show you how to be more positive about who you are and honour your connection to the Universe. In fact, all the rituals and practices in this section will bring you joyful relating, harmonious living and a true sense of happiness.

# The Key

Remember, your birth-chart or horoscope is like the key to a treasure chest containing the most precious jewels that make you you. Learn about them, and care for them well. Use this book to polish, nurture, respect and give value to the beautiful gemstones of who you are, and, in doing so, bring your potential to life. It's your right to be true to who you are, just by virtue of being born on this planet, and therefore being a child of Mother Earth and the cosmos.

Care for you, and you care for the Universe.

## TAURUS
## WORDS OF WISDOM

As you embark on your self-care journey, it's important to look at the lunar cycles and specific astrological moments throughout the year. At those times (and, indeed, at any time you choose), the words of Taurus wisdom below will be invaluable, empowering you with positive energy. Taking a few mindful moments at each of the four major phases of every lunar cycle and at the two important astrological moments in your solar year (see Glossary, p. 111) will affirm and enhance your positive attitude towards caring about yourself and the world.

**NEW CRESCENT MOON – to care for yourself:**

'All my senses delight me, and I know the Earth embraces me in her arms.'

'I affirm my creativity is a gift that I must treasure.'

'If I am sure of my purpose, then I can achieve great things.'

**FULL MOON – for sealing your intention to care for your feeling world:**

'I must be more adaptable and accept that other people have feelings.'

'If I connect to the natural world, I will open myself up to the joy of being.'

'When I go deep into myself, I discover what it is I actually desire.'

**WANING MOON – for letting go, and letting things be:**

'I must let my intuition guide me, rather than try to control my thoughts.'

'I will no longer equate love with possession.'

'I will let bygones be bygones and not hold grudges.'

**DARK OF THE MOON to acknowledge your 'shadow' side:**

'When I think I know best, I must consider other people's opinions, too.'

'I acknowledge the wild, rampaging Bull inside, who needs to express itself through art or love.'

'I will try to resist calculating every outcome in advance and live for the moment.'

**SOLAR RETURN SALUTATION – welcoming your new solar year to be true to who you are:**

Repeat on your birthday: 'My common sense and creativity are my gifts, and when both are employed for the good of the planet Earth, I am being true to my individuality.'

**SUN IN OPPOSITION – learn to be open to the opposite perspective that lies within you.**

Repeat when the sun is in Scorpio: 'My opposite sign is Scorpio, a sign of emotional determination and deep insight. These attributes are in my birth-chart, too. I must learn to be more aware and understanding of the feelings of others and allow more passion into my life.'

# The Taurus Personality

♉

*Beauty without the beloved is like a sword through the heart.*

**Dante Gabriel Rossetti, English poet and painter**

**Characteristics:** Artistic, sensuous, loyal, down to earth, reliable, practical, affectionate seductive, possessive, envious, determined, controlling, creative, Nature-loving, resourceful, dependable, dogmatic, luxury-loving, persistent, self-indulgent, kind-hearted, intolerant

**Symbol:** the Bull
In the ancient mythologies of Mesopotamia and Egypt, the constellation Taurus was a sacred bull, associated with agricultural calendars to define the period of spring to summer. The Greek god Zeus disguised himself as the magnificent white bull to abduct Europa, and we can see this as a metaphor for Taurus' gift of seduction, while the well-known

story of the dreaded Minotaur (with the head and tail of a bull and body of a man) resonates with the intolerance of the Taurus psyche.

**Planetary ruler:** Venus
With volcanic plains, ridged plateaus and hot mountains, Venus' surface is shrouded in thick clouds of odorous sulphuric acid. Hotter than Mercury, temperatures average 475°C. Rotating on its axis in the opposite direction to most of the other planets in the solar system, here on Venus the sun rises in the west, and sets in the east.

Astrological Venus: associated with feminine power, beauty and love. In the birth-chart, it describes the way we take pleasure, give love, care about ourselves and others, not forgetting how creative we are, whether we produce 'offspring' of the mind or the body. It also describes our own self-image, our vanity or our modesty.

**Element:** Earth
Like the other Earth signs, Virgo and Capricorn, Taurus is grounded in reality and skilled at managing and using resources. Earth signs are sensual, dependable and need to be engaged with or in some form of control of the material world.

**Modality:** Fixed
Sure of their purpose, but often stubborn to the
point of persistent inflexibility, the Bull makes sure
nothing can throw them off course or disrupt their
calculated plans.

**Body:** Throat, neck, cervical spine, shoulders

**Crystal:** Emerald

**Sun-sign profile:** A lover of beauty, luxury and the
good things in life, sensual Taurus is one of the most
affectionate and reliable signs of the zodiac.
However, the Bull has a tendency to indulge,
especially when it comes to good food, material
possessions and money. The Taurean has an eye not
only for beauty, but also for what could be of value
to them in the future – whether that's a fine painting
or the perfect partner.

The acquisitive Bull is a fanatical collector of objects
to show off their status and to boost their self-
worth. For example, all the spices known on the
planet might fill their kitchen, their balconies might
overflow with pot plants, they'll wear designer
clothes, if they can afford to (or copies, if not) and
they have incredible taste for colour, design and
decor in the home.

Taureans are usually out and about or working in the great outdoors, maybe running landscape-gardening courses or leading bands of hikers across the hills. Equally, they may be in front of an easel or a canvas or crafting in a pottery studio. With an innate awareness of the rhythms of Nature and an appreciation for the beauty of the world around them, no other sign in the zodiac is closer to the Earth itself than Taurus.

**Your best-kept secret:** For all your love of the tried and trusted, there is a wild, rampaging side to you, which often surprises even you, when you suddenly develop a passion for art, Nature or romance.

**What gives you meaning and purpose in life?**
Stability and a roof over your head. As long as you are in control of the tangible aspects of life, what matters to you is to create a beautiful, reliable world around you.

**What makes you feel good to be you?** Security, being rich enough to do what you like, feeling pampered, beautiful objects, people, music, good food, champagne, a garden of your own, a beautiful home, watching the sun rise or set

**What or who do you identify with?** Valuable antiques and artwork, auctioneers, bankers, stockbrokers, investors, musicians, dancers, artists, gardeners, hearty food and cooking, aesthetics, conservation, Nature, backpackers, ecological warriors

**What stresses you out?** Empty promises, being rushed, being told what to do, unpredictable people, not having enough money, those who don't value what you do, commercialisation, bad haircuts, cheap food

**What relaxes you?** Gardening, walking, painting, knitting, crafting, music, art appreciation, retail therapy, decorating your home, serene environments, walking across beautiful landscapes

**What challenges you?** Accepting your wild side, other people's opinions, double meanings, ambiguity, vagueness, not getting your way

# What Does Self-Care Mean For Taurus?

For the Bull, what matters most is leading a good, stable, pleasurable life. Being ruled by self-indulgent and body-conscious Venus, it's highly likely that you stick to your beauty and self-pampering routines, but also have moments of complete hedonistic indulgence in all the guilty pleasures of life. Now Venus (aka Aphrodite) was not only the goddess of love – she was also vain, envious and a tad manipulative, concocting love potions to win mortal men's hearts. Similarly seductive and sensual, the Bull knows how to attract others. But sometimes they are more determined to prove something to other people by the way they look than to care about their deeper self. So with this book, you can take great delight in discovering more about your innate potential, and loving all aspects of you.

# Self-Care Focus

In fact, the self-care practices in this book will inspire you to be who you are, and to make the best of your amazing skills, qualities and talents. They will show you how to care for and nurture the Taurus spirit of creativity and enterprise, to understand how to enrich your life, to free yourself from possessiveness and to let others be as they are.

Most of all, Taurus is a sign of gentleness and sensuality, a sign who is intuitively in touch with the natural world and the cosmos. By connecting to this innate earthiness, you will begin to see how resource-ful you really are and be able to accomplish anything you set out to achieve. Inner wealth is priceless, so begin to value yourself not for what you own or possess, but for the integrity and authenticity you find within yourself.

# PART ONE

# Caring For Your Mind And Feelings

Beauty is a mystery, but no one knows it any more. The recipes, the secrets are forgotten.

Edgar Degas, French artist

This section will inspire you to delight in your thoughts, express your ideas and take pleasure in your feelings. Once you get that deep sense of awareness of who you are and what you need, not only will it feel good to be alive, but you will be even more content to be yourself. The rituals and practices here will boost your self-esteem, motivate you to lead a more serene existence and enhance all forms of relationships with others. The most important relationship of all, with yourself, will be nurtured in the best possible way according to your sun sign.

Now, you may be that Bull who prefers a simple, back-to-Nature lifestyle, where you feel connected to the Earth and have little need of the politics of business or finances. Or you may be a more creative, enterprising Taurus, who builds a mini empire around yourself to feel secure. Whichever you are, empowering your mind with self-belief, creative inspiration and practical know-how will bring out the best in you. Caring for your mind and feelings is the best investment you can make in the present for your long-term security.

Quality matters to you, and it's the quality of the deeper feelings you discover in yourself that is most priceless and precious. The following practices will help you to understand better what feeds your Taurus mind and nurtures your feeling world, and, in expressing your true potential, to become who you truly are.

..............................................................

# BIRTH – OF – VENUS VISUALISATION

✳

Botticelli's painting, *The Birth of Venus*, is an evocative icon of the Taurus love of beauty, with its timeless image of an idealised Venus. The wind, Zephyr, has blown her to some exotic shore, and his companion – Aura, the nymph of spring – greets her, ready to cloak her nakedness.

**You will need:**
* A copy of a *Birth of Venus* image to focus on

**1.** Gaze at the image and imagine yourself as Venus, floating on the sea in your shell, the winds blowing you to an unknown shore.

**2.** Be aware of your nakedness as you cover your body with your hair and hands, and the cloak of the manifest world comes to shield you.

**3.** Step on to the land, walk on the grass, be aware of the ground beneath you. Feel how solid, reliable and warming it is, and indulge in the sensual delights of planet Earth and the pleasures of the landscape filled with joyful nymphs.

Being true to Venus isn't just about beauty and romance; it's also about feeling at one with Nature. So any time you're looking for creative inspiration, turn to this image of Venus, because her birth is yours, too. You can also focus on it whenever you need to feel special or to boost your self-esteem.

........................................................

## BOX OF TREASURE

♡

Taureans have many creative talents. Yet there are times when you doubt yourself or find it hard to knuckle down when inspiration is lacking. To vitalise your self-value and give yourself inspiration, create this treasure chest filled with encouraging words and empowering energy. Then you can dip into it any time of day or night.

**You will need:**

* Some small scraps or slips of paper or card and a pen
* Any beautiful box or container of your choice
* A handful of small tumbled citrine crystals
* A handful of small tumbled rose-quartz crystals
* A handful of small pieces of clear quartz
* A handful of small tumbled red carnelians

**1.** Write on your scraps of paper some creative ideas or future projects you would like to achieve – large or small. Or you can write down things, people or events that inspire you – such as 'oak tree' or 'antique furniture' or 'herb garden' and so on. There can be as many as you like, and you can always add more as you remove others.

**2.** Fold the papers up and fill your box with a mixture of the papers and your crystals.

**3.** As you fill the box, stir the contents with your hand gently and say:

> Citrine will bring creative voice,
> Rose quartz reveal my talent.
> Clear quartz to feel empowered and ready,
> Carnelian to energise and take action.

Whenever you need a boost of creative inspiration, simply put your hand in the box and pull out a slip of paper. Whatever the clue you read, hold the idea in your mind, and let it grow and develop into your next work in progress.

. . . . . . . . . . . . . . . . . . . . . . . . . . . . . . . . . . . . . . . . . . . . . . . . . . . .

## LEAVE YOUR MARK

★★
★

Emerald is the traditional Taurus birthstone, representing self-belief and inner wealth. The Roman emperor Nero was said to have gazed at his reflection in a huge emerald to bestow magnificence upon himself and to make a statement.

Making a statement matters to Taurus, too: you want your exotic perfume to waft in the air as you walk into or out of a room; you love to cook up the most memorable meal for your guests; or show off your garden. Here's a ritual to enable you to leave your mark and showcase your next brilliant idea.

**You will need:**
* An outdoor space where you can sit and observe green grass, trees, leaves or plants
* A rough green emerald

**1.** Go to you chosen spot and stand facing the greenery of your choice. (Being in a 'green' landscape will amplify the power of the emerald as it vibrates to and reflects this grounding energy.)

**2.** Hold the emerald up to your third-eye chakra (located between your eyebrows) and focus for a minute or so on the distant green of the landscape. Next, turn your attention to the green of the emerald. See in your mind how the green stone and the green landscape reflect one another.

**3.** Say: 'With this emerald I will make a lasting, enduring testament of my creative self'.

**4.** Now move the emerald from your forehead and just hold it in your hand, while repeating the statement in the previous step.

Keep the emerald in your workplace or in your pocket for one lunar cycle, and very soon you will be turning heads – in the best possible way.

.........................................................

## SHADES OF GREY

∗

The Bull's perception of life is either black or white, and it seems there's no room for shades of grey. The nuances and undercurrents of emotions, the subtleties of tangled relationships don't fit with their either-or world view.

Try this simple practice to discover that you do, in fact, have your own shades of grey, and to appreciate the nuances of feeling that run through you.

**You will need:**
* Black paint
* White paint
* A piece of paper or canvas
* A clear quartz crystal

**1.** With your paints, mix up a selection of different greys, from the darkest to the lightest.

**2.** On your paper or canvas, paint some black horizontal lines.

**3.** Between the black lines, paint each shade of grey – like a colour chart, starting with the darkest at the bottom, up to the lightest at the top.

49

**4.** Close your eyes and imagine there are even more shades and nuances of grey than you have managed to paint. In fact, how many do you think there are? Consider this for a moment in relation to the world and all the people in it. Perhaps for every shade of grey you have painted, there are thousands more in between?

**5.** With your eyes still closed, randomly place the crystal on one of the grey lines.

**6.** Open your eyes and focus on whichever grey the crystal is on. Reflect on how different it is from all the others; there's no ambiguity about it – it has its own identity.

**7.** Now look into the crystal and what do you see? Not just white or black, but endless shades and hues, refracted light, all part of the crystal.

Similarly, let the different shades of life and love (and emotions) be what they are. If you accept that grey is made up of both black and white, you will soon realise that the nuanced feelings that flow through you are made up of black and white, too.

## UNDERSTANDING THE BULL IN YOU

♡

The ancient symbol of the Bull has always represented strength, abundance and virility. Worshipped as both a solar and lunar influence in agriculture and fertility rites, the Taurus Bull has been particularly associated with the story of the Minotaur in Greek mythology. Briefly, King Minos of Crete made a deal with the god Poseidon that he would gift his most precious white bull to the god, if the king was given power over the sea. However, the greedy Minos reneged on the deal, wanting to keep his best bull for himself. Poseidon, in revenge, asked Aphrodite to curse King Minos' wife, Pasiphae, with unrelenting lust for the white bull. Eventually, Pasiphae managed to mate with the creature, and their offspring was the Minotaur, half bull, half man. This terrifying creature had an insatiable hunger for human flesh.

The Minotaur was hidden away in the famous labyrinth, feeding on the humans thrown in by King Minos. However, the hero Theseus killed the Minotaur with the help of the king's daughter Ariadne, who gave him a ball of thread to help him find his way out of the labyrinth. Like the Minotaur, one side of Taurus has a greedy nature, yet the innocent white bull in Taurus can flounder in other people's demands.

Here's how to accept the many facets of yourself, as symbolised by this myth.

**You will need:**
* A piece of paper and a pen

**1.** Write down the following list on your piece of paper:
   * King Minos – greedy
   * Poseidon – betrayed
   * Aphrodite – vengeful
   * White Bull – innocent
   * Minotaur – hungry
   * Pasiphae – obsessed
   * Theseus – heroic
   * Ariadne – clear-headed

**2.** Reflect on the words above and the myth. Ask yourself if you identify with any of those words or characters. Be honest.

Taurus can be betrayed (Poseidon), but then seek revenge (your inner Aphrodite). You can be innocent and pure (white bull), yet voracious (Minotaur) when driven by desire. You are also ready to be a hero (Theseus), who has to find their way through life where all is black and white, not a muddle of labyrinthine greys.

Yet you're also a lot like Ariadne, who offers the ball of thread with true compassion to show others the way.

If you can consider these different facets of your psyche without judgment or self-reproach, you are well on your way to synthesising them to be the best you can be. Caring about these aspects of yourself will uplift your mind, while bringing you acceptance of others and an ability to be the best of yourself.

........................................................................

## SELF – LOVE

✦✦
✦

In her orbit around the zodiac, your ruler, planet Venus, creates an extraordinary geometrical pattern due to her eight-year retrograde cycle (when a planet appears to move backwards, stations, then moves forwards again) mapped as a five-petalled rose. This rose pentagram aligns with one of the most important attributes of self-love. The rose pentagram is a perfect symbol for you to remind yourself to care for your loving qualities, restore positivity and practise self-nurturing.

**You will need:**
* A pentagram made up of 5 rose-petal shapes – you can either draw this or find an image online
* A mirror
* 5 rose-quartz crystals
* 5 rose petals
* 5 drops of ylang-ylang essential oil

**1.** Place the pentagram in front of your mirror.

**2.** Place a rose-quartz crystal and a rose petal in each segment of the pentagram.

**3.** Drip a drop of oil on to each crystal.

**4.** Gaze into the mirror, and say:

> With the power of Venus, I am blessed with
> positive qualities and love myself for all that I am.
> My talents will bloom like the rose and enable me
> to become who I really am.

Perform this ritual every new crescent moon to care for
your loving Taurus self.

...........................................................

## BEE IN YOUR BONNET

✳

Serene, sensuous and luxury-loving, the Bull is said to be the most patient and gentle of signs. And yes, you are, when things are going smoothly and your way. Which brings us back to 'grey areas' and, more importantly, zero tolerance.

Here's how to be a little more tolerant and accepting of other people's opinions. Acceptance of others means you are beginning to see life from a less subjective perspective and that's caring for your deeper self.

Visualise a beehive. There are bees going out and coming in all day long, like the busy thoughts in your head. One bee, on its journey to its favourite flower, is attracted by a brightly coloured one tucked into the gardener's hat, left on his bench. The bee buzzes down to check it out just before the gardener puts his hat back on. The bee is now in his bonnet. The bee didn't ask to be there, nor did the gardener invite it. So without getting in a tizz, the gardener takes off the hat, lays it gently on the bench, and the bee flies away. The gardener knows he has managed to save the buzzing bee and can now get back to his own important tasks.

Similarly, if you can drop the bee-in-the-bonnet attitude and be more accepting that other people have their own buzzing around to do, all your plans and schemes will transform into a veritable hive of positive activity.

# Relationships

For nostalgic Taureans, family means everything, and they are keen to pass down traditions and customs to the next generation. Loyal to friends and family, the Bull will do anything for anyone, but sometimes in their attempt to be generous to a fault, they forget that others have their own ways of doing things, too.

In love, the Bull adores all the conventional and romantic rules of the mating game. They dress the part, douse themselves in beauty products and indulge in their love of the traditional pleasures of romance – candlelit dinners, champagne, log fires and the like. This Fixed Earth sign wants a dedicated, loyal relationship, and although they can be slow to commit to long-term love, when they fall head over heels for someone, they can turn into the most passionate, rampaging and, often, possessive Bull. A Taurean makes a devoted partner who will do just about anything for the love of their life. And if their partner is as loyal and true as they are, then they'll always be there, as both friend and lover.

The way to a Bull's heart is through their stomach, and on first dates a home-cooked meal could be a deal breaker, as it proves to them that the focus of their desire really does care and want to pamper them. In fact, the

Bull needs stability more than they let on; they have to feel safe, and so instinctively look for partners who are good with finances, have an interest in property and know the difference between a bull and a bear market. Just like building a sense of financial security around them, a relationship is an investment to Taurus. If a risk in love is worth taking, they will be there for life.

. . . . . . . . . . . . . . . . . . . . . . . . . . . . . . . . . . . . . . . . . . . . . . . . . . . . . . . .

## CELTIC LOVE KNOT

♡

The Celtic love knot was a symbol of eternal love, and usually exchanged at prenuptial ceremonies using woven straw or ribbons. Sometimes the motif was engraved on copper rings or on a stone. The love feast was usually celebrated during a waxing moon, and the knot left during the full moon to draw down the positive lunar energy for fulfilment and fertility.

Perform this magical knot charm during a full moon to ensure fidelity and long-term commitment (the keys to a happy Taurus heart).

**You will need:**
* 2 red candles
* An image of a Celtic love knot (you can either copy one on to a piece of paper or a stone or purchase a ready-made, woven one)
* 2 rings
* A 15cm (6 inch) length of red ribbon

**1.** On the evening of a full moon, place your two candles on a table and light them.

**2.** Place your knot between the lit candles.

**3.** Take the two rings and thread the ribbon through each of them, then tie off in a knot.

**4.** Lay the looped rings on top of the love knot and say:

> With these two rings we will be one
> United in our destiny
> With lover's knots and tied be done
> Forever true for you and me.

Leave your knot and rings overnight to charge with the lunar power and activate the magic of long-term love.

......................................................

## BEING CAREFREE

♡

Taureans can be terribly self-conscious, often worrying about what others will think of them and seeking reassurance to feed their lack of self-esteem: 'I can't possibly go out looking like this', or, 'Hey, look at me. Do you like my new shoes?'

It's all very well taking seriously the impression you give in life, but sometimes you need to free up your inhibitions, care less about what others think and liberate your carefree side. Every Taurus has one, it's just a question of accessing it.

In Welsh legend, Rhiannon was a gracious lady who rode a white stallion, appearing magically from some otherworld. A Welsh prince chased after her, and it was only when he asked for her hand in marriage that she turned around, reassured that she was truly loved. Rhiannon was also a wild moon and Earth goddess, and sacred to her were songbirds, horses, sage and lavender. Her two identities are motifs in your own Taurus myth of the need for others to feed your self-esteem, alongside a realisation that you don't have to be dependent on other people's praise if you free up your wilder, carefree self. Here's how to give life to the moon and Earth goddess within.

**You will need:**

* A pin
* A white candle
* A handful of sage leaves
* Lavender essential oil
* A moonstone

**1.** On the evening of a full moon, take the pin and scratch or carve a symbol of the moon at the top of the candle.

**2.** Light the candle and place the sage leaves in front of it.

**3.** Drizzle a few drops of lavender oil over the leaves.

**4.** Place the moonstone on the sage leaves and reflect for a moment on the flame before you.

**5.** Now say:

> This moonstone shows my heart is sure.
> This sage it opens freedom's door.
> This candle lights my carefree soul
> This lavender lets self-love unfold.

**6.** Let the candle burn down, until it begins to melt the symbol of the moon.

**7.** After you have focused on the flame for a few minutes and have reflected on your intention, blow the candle out and leave overnight to charge the moonstone with lunar energy.

Take the moonstone with you when you go out and about to remind you of the uninhibited moon and Earth goddess within, who doesn't need other people's praise or reassurance to give her self-value.

........................................................................

## SEDUCTIVE POWER

♡

Dressed in perfumed garments and embroidered robes, adorned with golden brooches, necklaces and earrings, Aphrodite was indeed the goddess of seduction. She also wore a magic girdle known as the 'cestus', woven with symbolic threads representing the powers of seduction, desire and passion. (In her role as the goddess of marriage, Hera borrowed this from Aphrodite when trying to reconcile quarrelling spouses or to inspire suitors to woo their brides.)

Here is a simple ritual to unleash your seductive Taurean power to attract admirers and to make the best of yourself. Perform this during a new crescent-moon phase.

**You will need:**
* A rose
* A pearl
* A white tea light
* An apple
* 4 drops of rose essential oil
* A 90cm (36 inch) length ribbon or braid (colour of your choice)

**1.** Place the rose and the pearl either side of the candle, and light it.

**2.** Cut the apple into quarters, and place two pieces beside the pearl and two beside the rose.

**3.** Drizzle the essential oil over the apple pieces.

**4.** Encircle all your ingredients with the ribbon, then say:
>    With this girdle I bind desire.
>    The rose for love, the apple for fire,
>    The pearl for joy, the oil to seduce,
>    The candle to bring me the best for myself.

**5.** Blow out the candle and leave the ritual in place overnight.

In the morning, respectfully dispose of the apple and rose and keep the pearl in a safe place to ensure you attract the right kind love to you.

........................................................

## THE EMPRESS AND THE FOOL

♡

The Empress in tarot is usually associated with Taurus. She's creative, a bit of an Earth mother and – identified with Venus – she likes to look good. She's also possessive and controlling. The antithesis of the Empress in tarot is the Fool. Spontaneous, unreliable, charming and idealistic, he doesn't have his feet on the ground, nor does he look where he is going. He just impulsively enjoys life, rather than trying to manage it.

The smart Taurean is realistic and reliable and follows traditional values to achieve and create the security they need. Yet, in doing so, they often assume their colleagues, family or friends must follow the same rules. In fact, it can become a big bone of contention for many people to convince the Bull they have their own individual desires and needs that may not be compatible.

By working with the extremes of energies of the Empress and the Fool, here's a way to be more open to other people's private lives and to see that when you are not trying to control them, your energy can be channelled into your own personal creativity.

**You will need:**

* Images of the two cards (the Empress and the Fool)
* A piece of paper and a pen

**1.** Place the two images side by side on the piece of paper.

**2.** On your paper, above the Empress, write 'Calculating'.

**3.** Above the Fool, write 'Spontaneous'.

**4.** Now swap the cards' positions. Can the Empress be spontaneous? Yes, if she sets aside her self-righteousness and sees the world through a wider lens, unclouded by prejudice. And can the Fool be calculating? Yes, if he starts looking at the Earth below him, rather than keep his head in the clouds.

As you reflect on these two extremes of energy, you can also begin to find them in yourself. Be open and more accepting of other people's values and see how if the Empress in you frees herself from the chains of rigidity, she can open her arms and embrace the Fool's more spontaneous quality of life. It might bring her – and you – a surprisingly new perspective on creativity, too.

PART TWO

# Caring For Your Body

Better keep yourself clean and bright; you are the window through which you must see the world.

George Bernard Shaw, Irish playwright

**H**ere, you will discover alternative ways to look after and nurture your body, not just as a physical presence, but its connection to mind and spirit, too. This section gives you a wide range of ideas, from using sun-sign crystals to protect your physical and psychic self to fitness, diet and beauty tips. There are specific chakra practices and yoga poses especially suited to your sun sign, not forgetting bath-time rituals and calming practices to destress you and nurture holistic wellbeing.

Sensually aware, the Bull stays in tune with their physical needs, and instinctively cares for their body. They just 'know' what exercise is right for them at any given time. Being realists, Taureans also know how to sustain and preserve their beauty, looks and fitness goals. They're likely to have a diet plan, a list of the best gyms in town, dates already scheduled with a personal trainer or yoga group and certainly either a bike, hiking boots or walking shoes in their hallway. In fact, the Taurean knows that it's important to keep an eye on their body beautiful, or they can end up overindulging in all the so-called good things in life.

## Fitness and Movement

With Taurus ruling the throat, neck, cervical spine and shoulders, the Bull's best exercise routines are those that maximise flexibility, stretch and support the upper cervical spine and neck areas and also enhance natural grace and poise. This could be anything from yoga, Pilates and dancing to a brisk walk.

The renowned Bull-like stamina of Taurus means you not only have a strong constitution, but are determined to achieve your fitness goals. Some astrological schools of thought say that Taurus is downright lazy. And yes, you can and will take your time to get that fitness programme started or put off going for a walk when you'd rather be painting a masterpiece. But once you engage in any practice, you won't give up on it until you've achieved your aim.

## GETTING IN THE SWING

Even though Taurus is happy to throw down their yoga mat in the same place every day, they also love to hike across the countryside or delight in the beauty of new landscapes. Whether it's walking in the hills or digging their garden, communing with Nature makes Taureans feel good to be alive.

**1.** Find a route that you like the look of, whether it's along a country lane, up a hillside or includes the view of a great landscape – it all adds to the pleasure principle that Taureans need to boost their physical health.

**2.** Set off with necessary items such as water, snack and mobile phone in a backpack. Keep your body symmetrical when you walk. Once you have established your rhythm, begin to swing each arm back and forth in time with the opposite leg: right leg forward, left arm forward; left leg forward, right arm forward. This is a fairly natural motion.

**3.** Raise the arms a little higher each time, until, eventually, you are raising each one high above your head before swinging it back down behind you again.

Keep it up for as long as you like, and you'll be exercising not only your lower body, but your core and upper-body muscles, too.

Practise this style of walking at least once a week, as it will burn more calories and work more muscles than an ordinary stroll. It's the perfect Taurus regimented style of exercising, but with a landscape thrown in!

..........................................................

## *YOGA: CAMEL POSE (USHTRASANA)*

Every sun sign has a yoga pose associated with the part of the body it's traditionally ruled by. For Taurus, the camel pose opens up your chest and neck area to enable you to give and receive love, express your personal truth and feel self-confident. On a physical level, this pose also flexes the hips, stretches the entire front of the body, chest, abdomen and throat and strengthens the back muscles, too, thus improving overall flexibility.

**1.** Kneel on the floor with your legs just a little apart, then lower your bottom down to your heels. Press your shins and the tops of your feet into the floor.

**2.** Now place your hands on the backs of your hips, and lift up your body, so your bottom is no longer touching your heels.

**3.** Inhale, lift up your chest and push your hips forwards.

**4.** Draw your shoulder blades back to extend this arched position. When you feel you can't lean back any further, reach your fingertips down as far as you can towards your heels. Lean your head back slowly as you reach for your feet. Don't worry if you only touch your legs.

**5.** Stay in this position for the duration of 3 complete, long in- and out-breaths.

Repeat the pose whenever you need to feel stretched and ready for the day ahead.

## DANCING ON TIPTOES

The Bull has a natural sense of grace and balance. To boost this equilibrium and enhance suppleness, good posture and, therefore, good flexibility, you can practise this simple dancing-on-tiptoes exercise whenever you have a moment to spare.

**1.** Take off your shoes, if possible, and stand up straight with your hands by your sides.

**2.** Focus on an object in the distance, as you take a few rounds of slow, calming breaths.

**3.** Raise your arms up to shoulder height, one in front of you and one behind, with fingers outstretched.

**4.** Now, flex your feet and rise up on to your toes; hold for 10 seconds, then let your heels back down to the ground again.

**5.** Repeat the above 5 times (to warm up the arches and toe joints) and then rise again and start to tiptoe forwards (with your arms still raised, to benefit your core and upper body).

**6.** Start to dance freely, still on tiptoes, keeping your balance and moving in time to your own rhythm (or play a little music in the background, if you so desire).

You don't have to do this for long – say, three to five minutes to begin with – to feel refined and polished, your body movement more graceful in everything you do.

# Nutrition

Known as the gourmets of the zodiac, Taureans are very much aware of their bodies' nutritional needs. However, because they love the good things in life and are also creatures of habit, changing an indulgent diet for a more refined one can be a problem for the Bull, who hates changing anything (except when they're getting the best currency conversion rate). Having said that, when they begin to feel the odd bulge – whether from the guilty pleasure of chocolate or spending their well-earned money in the finest restaurants in town – the disciplined Bull charges into action, avoiding all the things they were previously addicted to. However, this nutritional pendulum swing between hedonism and sobriety means the Bull's body weight may be up and down, too.

Here are a couple of ways to keep a check and balance on healthy eating.

........................................................................

## TAURUS FOOD MANTRA

✳

Apart from getting on those scales every day, a mindful way to keep a check on your figure, nutritional needs and how much you really need to eat is to face yourself naked in the mirror once a week and repeat the following Taurus mantra:

> I love to indulge in all the luxuries of life, and that is who I am. I also know that to look good, to feel good, is to be aware of nutritional value and to use it to love my body.

Then, scrawl on the mirror with your lipstick (or a thick wipeable pen) what you see or feel before you. It may be 'bloated', 'pimple', 'looking good', 'no more sugar', 'quit the booze' and so on. Whatever the case, in these spontaneous moments of gazing in the mirror, you are setting yourself a Taurean task for, say, the week ahead – to improve, remedy or just carry on the good work, depending on the nutritional statement you have made.

When you next intentionally face yourself in the mirror – for the purposes of this exercise – see if the scrawl you made is still relevant. Have you managed to overcome the problem if there was one? Are you feeling better about your weight or food habits? If things have improved, write a brief congratulatory statement, and maybe even a replacement statement with something new to work on. If not, resolve to try harder with a morale booster and your Taurean persistence to get into the shape you want.

This simple practice will help you to keep an eye on your weight, while simultaneously reminding you of your body's nutritional needs.

..........................................................................

# HERB POTS

✳

Taureans love gardening because it gives them a sense of connection to the Earth and land, as well as the seasonal rituals of life on which they thrive. Nurturing the land will make you feel cared for by the Earth, and you will be caring for your nutritional needs, too.

Place a pot or planter of herbs on your window ledge, where you can harvest them quickly and easily. The herbs most suited to Taureans' nutritional needs are sage, rosemary, mint and thyme:

* Sage – packed with antioxidants, it aids brain function and the immune system, while improving oral health and digestion
* Rosemary – a good source of iron and vitamin B6 and reduces nasal congestion
* Thyme – a good source of vitamin C and also has anti-microbial properties
* Mint – aids IBS and many other digestive problems

Once your herbs are established, harvest them as needed (regularly snipping off any flower buds will encourage new leaf growth), and use freely in most culinary dishes to support all of the above (in particular, the often overindulged Taurean digestive system).

## Beauty

Now as we have seen, the Bull can swing between hedonism or sobriety, careful crafting or rampant romance. And when it comes to beauty, there are two Taurus types. One's bathroom cabinet overflows with hair products, face creams, skin moisturisers, jade rollers and all the latest tricks of the trade; the other – the Earth-mother type – loves the simple life, uses only sustainable products, buys organic and, while still concerned about their looks, will make their own avocado face masks and may even experiment with mud from their garden.

Whether you're into the most up-to-date beauty-care products and routines or prefer the simplicity of natural ones, use the following rituals to bring out the best of your stunning sensuality, and be either a true Earth mother or a fashionista.

........................................................................

## OAK-TREE BATH

♡

As rooted to the ground as the mighty oak, Taurus has long been associated with the myths of this splendid tree. One ancient Celtic folk belief held that if you saw a bull and then rubbed your hands on the trunk of an oak tree, your health would improve dramatically; another alleged that dew found on the grass under the tree was a magical beauty aid.

The following bath ritual will bring your Taurean aura a sense of peace and calm, while the magic of the oak makes your whole body beautiful.

**You will need:**
* Bath products of your choice
* A handful of lavender flowers
* Lavender essential oil
* An acorn, oak leaf or image of an oak tree

**1.** Run your bath and add your chosen products.

**2.** Sprinkle the lavender flowers over the water, along with a few drops of lavender oil.

**3.** Place the acorn, leaf or oak image at the foot end of the bath.

**4.** Now get into the bath and relax for a few minutes.

**5.** Focus on the oak motif and say, 'I am as strong as the oak tree, and as beautiful as its branches, leaves, trunk and roots'.

**6.** Cup some water in your hands and scatter it over your body. Imagine it is the dew beneath an oak tree, restoring your beauty.

After your bath, keep the acorn, oak leaf or image in a safe place. Repeat this ritual whenever you feel in need of a complete inner and outer beauty makeover.

## SACRED TO VENUS

♡

The rose, dove and myrtle flower are all sacred to Venus, your ruler, and in Roman mythology the swan, too, became one of her symbols. This simple ritual will make you feel as charismatic as the goddess herself, giving you a magical glow wherever you go.

**You will need:**
* A bowl of water
* Rose essential oil
* Myrtle essential oil
* A rose-quartz crystal (associated with the swan)
* A clear quartz crystal (associated with the dove)

**1.** Place the bowl of water in front of you on a table.

**2.** Sprinkle a few drops of each of the essential oils into the water, swirling it with your finger a little to disperse them.

**3.** Place the two crystals in the water and hold them below the surface in each hand for about 30 seconds to imbue you with Venus' sacred charisma.

**4.** Remove the crystals and keep them in a safe place for future use.

You will be filled with the radiance of the goddess herself and step out into the big, wide world knowing you are glowing with a glamorous Taurean aura.

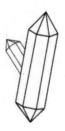

# CHAKRA BALANCE

The body's chakras are the epicentres of the life-force energy flowing through all things (see p. 22).

Taurus is traditionally associated with the throat chakra, located at the base of the throat and the centre for thought, communication, music, speech, art and writing. It vibrates to the colour blue.

When this chakra is underactive, you lose focus and lack direction and all forms of creative thought becomes jumbled or confused. To boost it, carry or wear lapis lazuli (the crystal of wisdom and creative thinking) to polish your mind and refresh old creative ideas or generate new ones. Once balanced, you will be musically or artistically inspired, your communication skills will improve and anything that you need to say will be said with confidence.

If you have an overactive throat chakra, you may treat other people with little respect and be intolerant of their opinions. Silly things will make you angry or frustrate you, and you will be filled with irrational and unrealistic ideas. To subdue an overactive throat chakra, wear or carry malachite, which enhances realistic thinking and tolerance, to ground and balance you.

# General Wellbeing

For all-round wellbeing, the following practices will create peace, comfort and that greatest of Taurus needs: a sense of security in their home and working lives.

Taurus thrives in a beautiful yet stable environment. Here, the bull's holistic health is nurtured by their instinctive synergy and interaction with their surroundings, and this in turn makes them feel at one with the world. So for all-round wellbeing, the following practices will create peace, comfort and that greatest of Taurus needs: a sense of security in their home and working lives.

........................................................................

## WELLBEING IN THE HOME

★★
★

The Taurean home and/or garden is usually the prettiest and most aesthetically pleasing of all their neighbours'. Cushions will be scattered in all the right places; the chosen colour scheme will create harmonious vibes; the garden will be filled with the most fragrant flowers or plants through each season of the year. But if you want to also create balanced, positive energy for yourself and your home, try harnessing the energy of the four astrological elements to help ground that Taurus energy and bring in a sense of security.

**You will need:**
* 4 candles – yellow (for air), blue (for water), red (for fire) and green (for earth)
* 4 crystals – citrine, blue lace agate, red carnelian and malachite

**1.** Light the four candles and place them in the shape of a square, with a candle at each corner.

**2.** Place the four crystals inside the square next to the candles, pointing inwards to the centre. (One crystal point will usually be more prominent than the others.)

**3.** Focus on your grid pattern and, taking up the crystals one at a time, say the relevant line for each of them:

* This citrine brings harmony to communication.
* This blue lace agate brings harmony to feelings.
* This red carnelian brings harmony to love.
* This malachite brings harmony to ground my intentions.

**4.** After a few minutes of quiet contemplation, blow out the candles to disperse the positive energy to all areas of your home.

Repeat this ritual whenever you need to boost a sense of wellbeing and harmony in the home.

. . . . . . . . . . . . . . . . . . . . . . . . . . . . . . . . . . . . . . . . . . . . . . . . . . . . . . . . . .

## DESTRESSING THE SENSES

✦✦
✦

The Bull stresses about money, people who rush them and, most of all, about not having a roof over their head. Being an Earth sign, Taurus is deeply aware of the five senses: sight, sound, touch, taste and smell; and this sensory meditation will calm you down whenever you feel bothered about, well, anything.

All you need to do is take five slow, deep, calming in- and out-breaths:

* During the first inhale/exhale, visualise five things you can see.
* During the second, visualise four things you can feel.
* During the third, visualise three things you can hear.
* During the fourth, visualise two things you can smell.
* During the fifth, visualise one thing you can taste.

If this doesn't work the first time around, try again until you get the hang of it. By the time you have visualised these sensory experiences, you will feel calmer, relaxed and stress-free.

# PART THREE

# Caring For
# Your
# Soul

Say not, 'I have found the path of my soul. Say rather, 'I have met the soul walking upon my path'. For the soul walks on all paths.

Kahlil Gibran, Lebanese–American writer and mystic

This final section offers you tailored, fun, easy and amazing ways to connect to and care for your sacred self. This, in turn, means you will begin to feel at one with the joyous energy of the Universe. You don't have to sign up to any religion or belief system (unless you want to) – just take some time to experience uplifting moments through your interaction with the spiritual aspects of the cosmos. Care for your sun sign's soul centre, and you care about the Universe, too.

Whether you talk to the trees, tend your cacti, stroke a cat or go beach-combing, it's that sense of being at one with Nature that brings Taureans a sense of spiritual joy. Wild woodlands, forests, even bleak landscapes and stone circles will appeal to the Taurean sense of the divine found in Nature. You might already be intrigued to follow up goddess beliefs, Wicca, natural magic and Druidism because they align with your deep connection to the ancient worship or celebration of the Earth. Nature is also where the Bull finds most contentment. This sense of being at peace with the world is often felt deep within, as they tune into the universal energy flow, manifesting as the gifts of the planet.

To care for your spiritual connection to the Universe and all that's in it, enjoy the following practices and discover your sacred self.

101

# A NATURE WALK

✳

It's not difficult for Taurus to engage with something divine that flows through all things, whether through animals, plants, rocks, the landscape or the weather. Known as animism, this spiritual essence is very much part of the Bull's experience of life, too, but that means balancing you with the energy of the world at large. Once you feel a sense of involvement, you will be caring for your sacred self, and the spirit within you will be alive, animated and joyful.

To really embrace and engage in this empowering spiritual energy, take an uplifting walk in Nature. Put on your hiking boots or sandals (depending on where you are going) and be mindful of each step along the way. Choose a route that might take in more than one kind of landscape. At each viewpoint, stand for a moment in silence and witness the light as it plays on the Earth, the stillness of the air or the wind as it whistles. As you listen, see, touch or smell the elements around you, be mindful of how this feels for you.

Through your senses – not forgetting your sixth sense (also known as your intuition) – you will feel truly at one with the Universe.

## CONNECT TO THE UNIVERSE

♡

If the Taurus soul is to be found through a connection to Nature, you can also go one step further and find an all-encompassing connection to the Universe to help you manifest your dreams. Maybe it's time to experience something deeper at work within you to be certain of that connection? (After all, Earth signs like tangible proof.)

Manifestation is about trusting in the Universe to help you achieve your goal. But to really make your goals reality, you must also believe that this universal energy flows through you, just as it flows through everything.

So if you truly believe, and have a true intention, try this visualisation to help you connect to your spiritual self, so you can begin to manifest the things you desire.

**1.** Imagine yourself standing in front of a closed door.

**2.** As you open the door, the light of the Universe streams into your mind, filling you with inspiration; all the hopes and dreams that you long for are suddenly real and viable, and they are right there before your eyes. See before you what your desire or intention is, and hold on to it.

**3.** Now step through the doorway and, in your mind, believe that you are literally embracing your intention, giving it life. Embrace also the belief in manifesting this desire, and your connection to the Universe will be sealed.

**4.** Come out of your visualisation and say, 'Thank you, Universe, for my gift of connection, where I also give goodness back to the Universe. My intention will manifest when the moment is right.'

You can repeat this visualisation at any time to inspire you to care for the sacred self within and to uplift and inspirit you with joy for being true to your Taurus psyche.

......................................................................

## THE MAGIC STONE

★★
 ★

Rocks, stones and crystals are all ways for Taurus to discover another way to connect to Nature.

The *omphalos* (meaning navel of the earth) is an ancient stone that was found at the oracle at Delphi in Greece. According to one Greek myth, Zeus asked two eagles to circle the Earth with a huge stone between the two of them, until they were told to drop it from the heavens to mark the centre of the Earth. It fell at Delphi.

Use the symbol of this ancient mystical stone to harness the power of your earthy mystique.

**You will need:**

* A large black stone to represent your *omphalos* (a piece of black obsidian, black tourmaline or similar) big enough to cup in your hands
* Cypress essential oil

**1.** Take your stone and anoint it with a little cypress oil to imbue it with positivity.

**2.** Stand outside, raise the stone to the sky and say, 'I am of the planets and heavens, the sky and the stone'.

**3.** Sit or kneel down and hold the stone down on the ground. As you do so, say, 'I am of the Earth, of the wildlife, the elements, the stone'.

**4.** Next, hold the stone close to your navel (the centre of yourself) and say, 'I am all of this Universe, this Nature and of myself, and this stone is my sacred connection to all'.

Keep your stone in a special place and, whenever you feel in need of a Taurean spiritual uplift, hold it to your navel and repeat the above.

# Last Words

Within these pages you'll have discovered how to draw on your innate Taurus potential to make your life what you want it to be. In fact, caring for yourself means you are beginning to be more aware of who you are and what truly makes you feel good to be you.

Living out your true potential means accepting your faults, as well as enhancing your virtues. And yes, you may also be too easily seduced by all forms of beauty, whether in the form of a romantic Adonis or a dazzling career, for example, but take a tip from your planetary goddess, Venus – there's nothing wrong with being a little vain or enchanting; both nurture Taureans' holistic wellbeing, which results in loving and caring for you.

You are, hopefully, discovering not only the best way to express your latent passion through your creativity, but also that there's no time like the present to enjoy being the practical, organised and deeply sensual Earth sign that you are. Nurturing your best qualities is like cultivating a garden. You do have to dig and rake and turn the soil before you plant anything, but through tending to your mind, your feelings, your body and soul, you will start to flourish. Then, with happiness and pride, you'll see the results of what you have planted. That is the joy of Taurus self-care.

So whichever kind of Bull you are – the back-to-Nature one or the enterprising, ambitious one – care about your passion, care about your delight in beauty and care about the seductive powers you have been blessed with. By loving all of you – the good and not-so-good qualities alike – you care for the goodness, beauty and joy of the planet, too. Be as kind to yourself as you are towards Nature, animals and other people, and that kindness will ensure you live out your potential to truly honour who you are becoming.

# Resources

Main sites for crystals, stones, candles, smudging sticks, incense, pouches, essential oils and everything needed for the holistic self-care practices included this book:

**holisticshop.co.uk**
**thepsychictree.co.uk**
**thesoulangels.co.uk**
**earthcrystals.com**
**livrocks.com**
**artisanaromatics.com**

For a substantial range of books (and metaphysical items) on astrology, divination, runes, palmistry, tarot and holistic health, etc.:

**thelondonastrologyshop.com**
**watkinsbooks.com**
**mysteries.co.uk**
**barnesandnoble.com**
**innertraditions.com**

For more information on astrology, personal horo-scopes and birth-chart calculations:
**astro-charts.com** (simplest, very user friendly)

**horoscopes.astro-seek.com**
(straightforward)
**astrolibrary.org/free-birth-chart**
(easy to use, with lots of extra information)

# Glossary

**Aura** An invisible electromagnetic energy field that emanates from and surrounds all living beings

**Auric power** The dominant colour of the aura that reveals your current mood or state

**Chakra** Sanskrit for 'wheel', in Eastern spiritual traditions the seven chakras are the main epicentres – or wheels – of invisible energy throughout the body

**Dark of the moon** This is when the moon is invisible to us, due to its proximity to the sun; it is a time for reflection, solitude and a deeper awareness of oneself

**Divination** Gaining insight into the past, present and future using symbolic or esoteric means

**Double-terminator crystal** A quartz crystal with a point at each end, allowing its energy to flow both ways

**Full moon** The sun is at its maximum opposition to the moon, thus casting light across all of the moon's orb; in esoteric terms, it is a time for culmination, finalising deals, committing to love and so on

**Geopathic stress** Negative energy emanating from and on the Earth, such as underground water courses, tunnels, overhead electrical cables and geological faults

**Grid** A specific pattern or layout of items symbolising specific intentions or desires

**Horoscope** An astrological chart or diagram showing the position of the sun, moon and planets at the time of any given event, such as the moment of somebody's birth, a marriage or the creation of an enterprise; it is used to interpret the characteristics or to forecast the future of that person or event

**New crescent moon** A fine sliver of crescent light that appears curving outwards to the right in the northern hemisphere and to the left in the southern hemisphere; this phase is for beginning new projects, new romance, ideas and so on

**Psychic energy** One's intuition, sixth sense or instincts, as well as the divine, numinous or magical power that flows through everything

**Shadow side** In astrology, your shadow side describes those aspects of your personality associated with your opposite sign and of which you are not usually aware

**Smudging** Clearing negative energy from the home with a smouldering bunch of dried herbs, such as sage

**Solar return salutation** A way to give thanks and welcome the sun's return to your zodiac sign once a year (your birthday month)

**Sun in opposition** The sun as it moves through the opposite sign to your own sun sign

**Sun sign** The zodiac sign through which the sun was moving at the exact moment of your birth

**Waning moon** The phase of the moon after it is full, when it begins to lose its luminosity – the waning moon is illuminated on its left side in the northern hemisphere, and on its right side in the southern hemisphere; this is a time for letting go, acceptance and preparing to start again

**Waxing moon** The phase between a new and a full moon, when it grows in luminosity – the waxing moon is illuminated on its right side in the northern hemisphere and on its left side in the southern hemisphere; this is a time for putting ideas and desires into practice

**Zodiac** The band of sky divided into twelve segments (known as the astrological signs), along which the paths of the sun, the moon and the planets appear to move

# About the Author

After studying at the Faculty of Astrological Studies in London, the UK, Sarah gained the Diploma in Psychological Astrology – an in-depth 3-year professional training programme cross-fertilised by the fields of astrology and depth, humanistic and transpersonal psychology. She has worked extensively in the media as astrologer for titles such as *Cosmopolitan* magazine (UK), *SHE, Spirit & Destiny* and the *London Evening Standard*, and appeared on UK TV and radio shows, including *Steve Wright in the Afternoon* on BBC Radio 2.

Her mainstream mind-body-spirit books include the international bestsellers, *The Tarot Bible, The Little Book of Practical Magic* and *Secrets of the Universe in 100 Symbols*.

Sarah currently practises and teaches astrology and other esoteric arts in the heart of the countryside.

# Acknowledgements

I would first like to thank everyone at Yellow Kite, Hodder & Stoughton and Hachette UK who were part of the process of creating this series of twelve zodiac self-care books. I am especially grateful to Carolyn Thorne for the opportunity to write these guides; Anne Newman for her editorial advice, which kept me 'carefully' on the right track; and Olivia Nightingall who kept me on target for everything else! It is when people come together with their different skills and talents that the best books are made – so I am truly grateful for being part of this team.

# See the full Astrology Self-Care series here

9781399704885  9781399704915  9781399704588

9781399704618  9781399704649  9781399704670

9781399704700  9781399704731  9781399704762

9781399704793  9781399704823  9781399704854

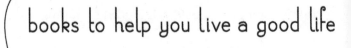

yellow
kite

books to help you live a good life

Join the conversation and tell
us how you live a #goodlife

@yellowkitebooks
YellowKiteBooks
Yellow Kite Books
YellowKiteBooks